The Poetry Of Anne Bradstreet

Volume 2 - Contemplations

Anne Bradstreet was born in 1612 in Northampton, England. Her parents position allowed them to educate Anne across many subjects which was unusual for its day. In her teens she contracted smallpox which was to undermine her health in later years.

She married Simon at the age of sixteen. They, along with her parents, emigrated to America with other Puritans in 1630 arriving on June 14th in Massachusetts. They moved south to Charlestown almost immediately to find better conditions. After a short stay they moved yet further south to help found the 'City on the Hill' Boston. By 1632 they had moved once more, this time to Cambridge, Massachusetts where Anne gave birth to her first child, Samuel.

The family was instrumental in setting up Harvard University in 1636 but by the early 1640's pregnant with her sixth child they moved for the sixth time to Andover Parish. In all Anne bore eight children although her health was always weak.

She did however write some beautiful poetry and in 1650, the Rev. John Woodbridge had her collection of verse; The Tenth Muse Lately Sprung Up in America composed by "A Gentlewoman from Those Parts" published in London, making Anne the first female poet ever published in both England and the New World.

On July 10, 1666, their North Andover family home burned down to leave them homeless. Tragically her own personal library of some 800 books was also lost in the flames. By now, Anne's health was slowly failing. She suffered from tuberculosis and had to deal with the loss of cherished relatives. But her will remained strong and faith in God undiminished.

Anne Bradstreet died on September 16, 1672 in North Andover, Massachusetts at the age of 60.

The Prologue

To sing of wars, of captains, and of kings,
Of cities founded, commonwealths begun,
For my mean pen are too superior things:
Or how they all, or each, their dates have run;
Let poets and historians set these forth,
My obscure lines shall not so dim their work.

But when my wondering eyes and envious heart
Great Bartas' sugared lines do but read o'er,
Fool I do grudge the Muses did not part
'Twixt him and me that overfluent store;
A Bartas can do what a Bartas will,

But simple I according to my skill.

From school-boys tongues no rhetoric we expect,
Nor yet a sweet consort from broken strings,
Nor perfect beauty where's a main defect:
My foolish, broken, blemished Muse so sings;
And this to mend, alas, no art is able,
'Cause nature made is so, irreparable.

Nor can I, like that fluent, sweet-tongued Greek
Who lisped at first, in future times speak plain;
By art he gladly found what he did seek
A full requitl of his striving pain.
Art can do much, but this maxim's most sure:
A weak or wounded brain admits no cure.

I am obnoxious to each carping tongue
Who says my hand a needle better fits.
A poet's pen all scorn I should thus wrong;
For such despite they cast on female wits,
If what I do prove well, it won't advance
They'll say it was stolen, or else it was by chance.

But shure the ancient Greeks were far more mild,
Else of our sex why feignéd they those Nine,
And Posey made Calliope's own child?
So 'mongst the rest they placed the Arts Divine.
But this weak knot they will full soon untie
The Greeks did naught but play the fools and lie.

Let Greeks be Greeks, and women what they are.
Men have precenency, and still excell.
It is but vain unjustly to wage war,
Men can do best, and women know it well.
Preëminence in all and each is yours
Yet grant some small acknowledgement of ours.

And oh, ye high flownquills that soar the skies,
And ever with your prey still catch your praise,
If e'er you deign these lowly lines your eyes,
Give thyme or parsley wreath; I ask no bays.
This mean and unrefinéd ore of mine
Will make your glistening gold but more to shine.

We May Live Together
If ever two were one, then surely we.

If ever man were lov'd by wife, then thee.
If ever wife was happy in a man,
Compare with me, ye women, if you can.
I prize thy love more than whole Mines of gold
Or all the riches that the East doth hold.
My love is such that Rivers cannot quench,
Nor ought but love from thee give recompetence.
Thy love is such I can no way repay.
The heavens reward thee manifold, I pray.
Then while we live, in love let's so persever
That when we live no more, we may live ever.

A Dialogue between Old England And New
New England.
Alas, dear Mother, fairest Queen and best,
With honour, wealth, and peace happy and blest,
What ails thee hang thy head, and cross thine arms,
And sit i' the dust to sigh these sad alarms?
What deluge of new woes thus over-whelm
The glories of thy ever famous Realm?
What means this wailing tone, this mournful guise?
Ah, tell thy Daughter; she may sympathize.

Old England.
Art ignorant indeed of these my woes,
Or must my forced tongue these griefs disclose,
And must my self dissect my tatter'd state,
Which Amazed Christendom stands wondering at?
And thou a child, a Limb, and dost not feel
My weak'ned fainting body now to reel?
This physic-purging-potion I have taken
Will bring Consumption or an Ague quaking,
Unless some Cordial thou fetch from high,
Which present help may ease my malady.
If I decease, dost think thou shalt survive?
Or by my wasting state dost think to thrive?
Then weigh our case, if 't be not justly sad.
Let me lament alone, while thou art glad.

New England.
And thus, alas, your state you much deplore
In general terms, but will not say wherefore.
What Medicine shall I seek to cure this woe,
If th' wound's so dangerous, I may not know?
But you, perhaps, would have me guess it out.
What, hath some Hengist like that Saxon stout

By fraud and force usurp'd thy flow'ring crown,
Or by tempestuous Wars thy fields trod down?
Or hath Canutus, that brave valiant Dane,
The regal peaceful Sceptre from thee ta'en?
Or is 't a Norman whose victorious hand
With English blood bedews thy conquered Land?
Or is 't intestine Wars that thus offend?
Do Maud and Stephen for the Crown contend?
Do Barons rise and side against their King,
And call in Foreign aid to help the thing?
Must Edward be depos'd? Or is 't the hour
That second Richard must be clapp'd i' th' Tower?
Or is it the fatal jar, again begun,
That from the red, white pricking Roses sprung?
Must Richmond's aid the Nobles now implore
To come and break the tushes of the Boar?
If none of these, dear Mother, what's your woe?
Pray, do not fear Spain's bragging Armado.
Doth your Ally, fair France, conspire your wrack,
Or doth the Scots play false behind your back?
Doth Holland quit you ill for all your love?
Whence is this storm, from Earth or Heaven above?
Is 't drought, is 't Famine, or is 't Pestilence?
Dost feel the smart, or fear the consequence?
Your humble Child entreats you shew your grief.
Though Arms nor Purse she hath for your relief
Such is her poverty, yet shall be found
A suppliant for your help, as she is bound.

Old England.
I must confess some of those Sores you name
My beauteous Body at this present maim,
But foreign Foe nor feigned friend I fear,
For they have work enough, thou knowest, elsewhere.
Nor is it Alcie's son and Henry's Daughter
Whose proud contention cause this slaughter;
Nor Nobles siding to make John no King,
French Louis unjustly to the Crown to bring;
No Edward, Richard, to lose rule and life,
Nor no Lancastrians to renew old strife;
No Crook-backt Tyrant now usurps the Seat,
Whose tearing tusks did wound, and kill, and threat.
No Duke of York nor Earl of March to soil
Their hands in Kindred's blood whom they did foil;
No need of Tudor Roses to unite:
None knows which is the Red or which the White.
Spain's braving Fleet a second time is sunk.

France knows how of my fury she hath drunk
By Edward third and Henry fifth of fame;
Her Lilies in my Arms avouch the same.
My Sister Scotland hurts me now no more,
Though she hath been injurious heretofore.
What Holland is, I am in some suspense,
But trust not much unto his Excellence.
For wants, sure some I feel, but more I fear;
And for the Pestilence, who knows how near?
Famine and Plague, two sisters of the Sword,
Destruction to a Land doth soon afford.
They're for my punishments ordain'd on high,
Unless thy tears prevent it speedily.
But yet I answer not what you demand
To shew the grievance of my troubled Land.
Before I tell the effect I'll shew the cause,
Which are my sins, the breach of sacred Laws:
Idolatry, supplanter of a Nation,
With foolish superstitious adoration,
Are lik'd and countenanc'd by men of might,
The Gospel is trod down and hath no right.
Church Offices are sold and bought for gain
That Pope had hope to find Rome here again.
For Oaths and Blasphemies did ever ear
From Beelzebub himself such language hear?
What scorning of the Saints of the most high!
What injuries did daily on them lie!
What false reports, what nick-names did they take,
Not for their own, but for their Master's sake!
And thou, poor soul, wast jeer'd among the rest;
Thy flying for the Truth I made a jest.
For Sabbath-breaking and for Drunkenness
Did ever Land profaneness more express?
From crying bloods yet cleansed am not I,
Martyrs and others dying causelessly.
How many Princely heads on blocks laid down
For nought but title to a fading Crown!
'Mongst all the cruelties which I have done,
Oh, Edward's Babes, and Clarence's hapless Son,
O Jane, why didst thou die in flow'ring prime?
Because of Royal Stem, that was thy crime.
For Bribery, Adultery, for Thefts, and Lies
Where is the Nation I can't paralyze?
With Usury, Extortion, and Oppression,
These be the Hydras of my stout transgression;
These be the bitter fountains, heads, and roots
Whence flow'd the source, the sprigs, the boughs, and fruits.

Of more than thou canst hear or I relate,
That with high hand I still did perpetrate,
For these were threat'ned the woeful day
I mocked the Preachers, put it fair away.
The Sermons yet upon record do stand
That cried destruction to my wicked Land.
These Prophets' mouths (all the while) was stopt,
Unworthily, some backs whipt, and ears crept;
Their reverent cheeks bear the glorious marks
Of stinking, stigmatizing Romish Clerks;
Some lost their livings, some in prison pent,
Some grossly fined, from friends to exile went:
Their silent tongues to heaven did vengeance cry,
Who heard their cause, and wrongs judg'd righteously,
And will repay it sevenfold in my lap.
This is fore-runner of my after-clap.
Nor took I warning by my neighbors' falls.
I saw sad Germany's dismantled walls,
I saw her people famish'd, Nobles slain,
Her fruitful land a barren heath remain.
I saw (unmov'd) her Armies foil'd and fled,
Wives forc'd, babes toss'd, her houses calcined.
I saw strong Rochelle yield'd to her foe,
Thousands of starved Christians there also.
I saw poor Ireland bleeding out her last,
Such cruelty as all reports have past.
Mine heart obdurate stood not yet aghast.
Now sip I of that cup, and just 't may be
The bottom dregs reserved are for me.

New England.
To all you've said, sad mother, I assent.
Your fearful sins great cause there 's to lament.
My guilty hands (in part) hold up with you,
A sharer in your punishment's my due.
But all you say amounts to this effect,
Not what you feel, but what you do expect.
Pray, in plain terms, what is your present grief?
Then let's join heads and hands for your relief.

Old England.
Well, to the matter, then. There's grown of late
'Twixt King and Peers a question of state:
Which is the chief, the law, or else the King?
One saith, it's he; the other, no such thing.
My better part in Court of Parliament
To ease my groaning land shew their intent

To crush the proud, and right to each man deal,
To help the Church, and stay the Common-Weal.
So many obstacles comes in their way
As puts me to a stand what I should say.
Old customs, new Prerogatives stood on.
Had they not held law fast, all had been gone,
Which by their prudence stood them in such stead
They took high Strafford lower by the head,
And to their Laud be 't spoke they held 'n th' Tower
All England's metropolitan that hour.
This done, an Act they would have passed fain
No prelate should his Bishopric retain.
Here tugg'd they hard indeed, for all men saw
This must be done by Gospel, not by law.
Next the Militia they urged sore.
This was denied, I need not say wherefore.
The King, displeased, at York himself absents.
They humbly beg return, shew their intents.
The writing, printing, posting to and fro,
Shews all was done; I'll therefore let it go.
But now I come to speak of my disaster.
Contention's grown 'twixt Subjects and their Master,
They worded it so long they fell to blows,
That thousands lay on heaps. Here bleeds my woes.
I that no wars so many years have known
Am now destroy'd and slaughter'd by mine own.
But could the field alone this strife decide,
One battle, two, or three I might abide,
But these may be beginnings of more woe
Who knows, the worst, the best may overthrow!
Religion, Gospel, here lies at the stake,
Pray now, dear child, for sacred Zion's sake,
Oh, pity me in this sad perturbation,
My plundered Towns, my houses' devastation,
My ravisht virgins, and my young men slain,
My wealthy trading fallen, my dearth of grain.
The seedtime's come, but Ploughman hath no hope
Because he knows not who shall inn his crop.
The poor they want their pay, their children bread,
Their woful mothers' tears unpitied.
If any pity in thy heart remain,
Or any child-like love thou dost retain,
For my relief now use thy utmost skill,
And recompense me good for all my ill.

New England.
Dear mother, cease complaints, and wipe your eyes,

Shake off your dust, cheer up, and now arise.
You are my mother, nurse, I once your flesh,
Your sunken bowels gladly would refresh.
Your griefs I pity much but should do wrong,
To weep for that we both have pray'd for long,
To see these latter days of hop'd-for good,
That Right may have its right, though 't be with blood.
After dark Popery the day did clear;
But now the Sun in's brightness shall appear.
Blest be the Nobles of thy Noble Land
With (ventur'd lives) for truth's defence that stand.
Blest be thy Commons, who for Common good
And thy infringed Laws have boldly stood.
Blest be thy Counties, who do aid thee still
With hearts and states to testify their will.
Blest be thy Preachers, who do cheer thee on.
Oh, cry: the sword of God and Gideon!
And shall I not on them wish Mero's curse
That help thee not with prayers, arms, and purse?
And for my self, let miseries abound
If mindless of thy state I e'er be found.
These are the days the Church's foes to crush,
To root out Prelates, head, tail, branch, and rush.
Let's bring Baal's vestments out, to make a fire,
Their Mitres, Surplices, and all their tire,
Copes, Rochets, Croziers, and such trash,
And let their names consume, but let the flash
Light Christendom, and all the world to see
We hate Rome's Whore, with all her trumpery.
Go on, brave Essex, shew whose son thou art,
Not false to King, nor Country in thy heart,
But those that hurt his people and his Crown,
By force expel, destroy, and tread them down.
Let Gaols be fill'd with th' remnant of that pack,
And sturdy Tyburn loaded till it crack.
And ye brave Nobles, chase away all fear,
And to this blessed Cause closely adhere.
O mother, can you weep and have such Peers?
When they are gone, then drown your self in tears,
If now you weep so much, that then no more
The briny Ocean will o'erflow your shore.
These, these are they (I trust) with Charles our king,
Out of all mists such glorious days will bring
That dazzled eyes, beholding, much shall wonder
At that thy settled Peace, thy wealth, and splendour,
Thy Church and Weal establish'd in such manner
That all shall joy that thou display'dst thy banner,

And discipline erected so, I trust,
That nursing Kings shall come and lick thy dust.
Then Justice shall in all thy Courts take place
Without respect of persons or of case.
Then bribes shall cease, and suits shall not stick long,
Patience and purse of Clients for to wrong.
Then High Commissions shall fall to decay,
And Pursuivants and Catchpoles want their pay.
So shall thy happy Nation ever flourish,
When truth and righteousness they thus shall nourish.
When thus in Peace, thine Armies brave send out
To sack proud Rome, and all her vassals rout.
There let thy name, thy fame, and valour shine,
As did thine Ancestors' in Palestine,
And let her spoils full pay with int'rest be
Of what unjustly once she poll'd from thee.
Of all the woes thou canst let her be sped,
Execute to th' full the vengeance threatened.
Bring forth the beast that rul'd the world with's beck,
And tear his flesh, and set your feet on's neck,
And make his filthy den so desolate
To th' 'stonishment of all that knew his state.
This done, with brandish'd swords to Turkey go,
(For then what is it but English blades dare do?)
And lay her waste, for so's the sacred doom,
And do to Gog as thou hast done to Rome.
Oh Abraham's seed, lift up your heads on high,
For sure the day of your redemption's nigh.
The scales shall fall from your long blinded eyes,
And him you shall adore who now despise.
Then fullness of the Nations in shall flow,
And Jew and Gentile to one worship go.
Then follows days of happiness and rest.
Whose lot doth fall to live therein is blest.
No Canaanite shall then be found 'n th' land,
And holiness on horses' bells shall stand.
If this make way thereto, then sigh no more,
But if at all thou didst not see 't before.
Farewell, dear mother; Parliament, prevail,
And in a while you'll tell another tale.

A Letter To Her husband
Absent upon Public Employment

My head, my heart, mine eyes, my life, nay more,
My joy, my magazine, of earthly store,

If two be one, as surely thou and I,
How stayest thou there, whilst I at Ipswich lie?
So many steps, head from the heart to sever,
If but a neck, soon should we be together.
I, like the Earth this season, mourn in black,
My Sun is gone so far in's zodiac,
Whom whilst I 'joyed, nor storms, nor frost I felt,
His warmth such fridged colds did cause to melt.
My chilled limbs now numbed lie forlorn;
Return; return, sweet Sol, from Capricorn;
In this dead time, alas, what can I more
Than view those fruits which through thy heart I bore?
Which sweet contentment yield me for a space,
True living pictures of their father's face.
O strange effect! now thou art southward gone,
I weary grow the tedious day so long;
But when thou northward to me shalt return,
I wish my Sun may never set, but burn
Within the Cancer of my glowing breast,
The welcome house of him my dearest guest.
Where ever, ever stay, and go not thence,
Till nature's sad decree shall call thee hence;
Flesh of thy flesh, bone of thy bone,
I here, thou there, yet both but one.

A Love letter To Her Husband
Phoebus make haste, the day's too long, begone,
The silent night's the fittest time for moan;
But stay this once, unto my suit give ear,
And tell my griefs in either Hemisphere:
(And if the whirling of thy wheels do n't drown'd
The woful accents of my doleful sound),
If in thy swift career thou canst make stay,
I crave this boon, this errand by the way:
Commend me to the man more lov'd than life,
Show him the sorrows of his widow'd wife,
My dumpish thoughts, my groans, my brackish tears,
My sobs, my longing hopes, my doubting fears,
And, if he love, how can he there abide?
My interest's more than all the world beside.
He that can tell the stars or Ocean sand,
Or all the grass that in the meads do stand,
The leaves in th' woods, the hail or drops of rain,
Or in a cornfield number every grain,
Or every mote that in the sunshine hops,
May court my sighs and number all my drops.

Tell him, the countless steps that thou dost trace,
That once a day thy spouse thou mayst embrace;
And when thou canst not treat by loving mouth,
Thy rays afar, salute her from the south.
But for one month I see no day (poor soul)
Like those far situate under the pole,
Which day by day long wait for thy arise,
O how they joy when thou dost light the skies.
O Phoebus, hadst thou but thus long from thine
Restrain'd the beams of thy beloved shine,
At thy return, if so thou couldst or durst,
Behold a Chaos blacker than the first.
Tell him here's worse than a confused matter,
His little world's a fathom under water,
Naught but the fervor of his ardent beams
Hath power to dry the torrent of these streams.
Tell him I would say more, but cannot well,
Opressed minds abrupted tales do tell.
Now post with double speed, mark what I say,
By all our loves conjure him not to stay.

An Apology
To finish what's begun, was my intent,
My thoughts and my endeavours thereto bent;
Essays I many made but still gave out,
The more I mus'd, the more I was in doubt:
The subject large my mind and body weak,
With many moe discouragements did speak.
All thoughts of further progress laid aside,
Though oft perswaded, I as oft deny'd,
At length resolv'd, when many years had past,
To prosecute my story to the last;
And for the same, I hours not few did spend,
And weary lines (though lanke) I many pen'd:
But 'fore I could accomplish my desire,
My papers fell a prey to th'raging fire.
And thus my pains (with better things) I lost,
Which none had cause to wail, nor I to boast.
No more I'le do sith I have suffer'd wrack,
Although my Monarchies their legs do lack:
Nor matter is't this last, the world now sees,
Hath many Ages been upon his knees.

An Epitaph On My Dear And Ever Honoured Mother Mrs. Dorothy Dudley, Who Deceased December 27 1643

A worthy Matron of unspotted life,
A loving Mother and obedient wife,
A friendly Neighbor, pitiful to poor,
Whom oft she fed, and clothed with her store;
To Servants wisely aweful, but yet kind,
And as they did, so they reward did find:
A true Instructer of her Family,
The which she ordered with dexterity.
The publick meetings ever did frequent,
And in her Closet constant hours she spent;
Religious in all her words and wayes,
Preparing still for death, till end of dayes:
Of all her Children, Children, liv'd to see,
Then dying, left a blessed memory.

Upon Some Distemper Of Body

In anguish of my heart replete with woes,
And wasting pains, which best my body knows,
In tossing slumbers on my wakeful bed,
Bedrenched with tears that flowed from mournful head,
Till nature had exhausted all her store,
Then eyes lay dry, disabled to weep more;
And looking up unto his throne on high,
Who sendeth help to those in misery;
He chased away those clouds and let me see
My anchor cast i' th' vale with safety.
He eased my soul of woe, my flesh of pain,
and brought me to the shore from troubled main.

As Spring The Winter Doth Succeed
May 13, 1657

As spring the winter doth succeed,
And leaues the naked Trees doe dresse,
The earth all black is cloth'd in green;
At svn-shine each their joy expresse.
My Svns returned with healing wings.
My Soul and Body doth rejoice;
My heart exvlts, and praises sings
To him that heard my wailing Voice.
My winters past, my stormes are gone,
And former clowdes seem now all fled;
But, if they mvst eclipse again,
I'le rvn where I was succoured.

I haue a shelter from the storm,
A shadow from the fainting heat;
I haue accesse vnto his Throne,
Who is a God so wondrous great.
O hast thou made my Pilgrimage
Thvs pleasant, fair, and good;
Bless'd me in Youth and elder Age,
My Baca made a springing flood?
I studiovs am what I shall doe,
To show my Duty with delight;
All I can giue is but thine own,
And at the most a simple mite.

As Weary Pilgrim Now At Rest
As weary pilgrim, now at rest,
Hugs with delight his silent nest
His wasted limbes, now lye full soft
That myrie steps, haue troden oft
Blesses himself, to think vpon
his dangers past, and travailes done
The burning sun no more shall heat
Nor stormy raines, on him shall beat.
The bryars and thornes no more shall scratch
nor hungry wolues at him shall catch
He erring pathes no more shall tread
nor wild fruits eate, in stead of bread,
for waters cold he doth not long
for thirst no more shall parch his tongue
No rugged stones his feet shall gaule
nor stumps nor rocks cause him to fall
All cares and feares, he bids farwell
and meanes in safity now to dwell.
A pilgrim I, on earth, perplext
wth sinns wth cares and sorrows vext
By age and paines brought to decay
and my Clay house mouldring away
Oh how I long to be at rest
and soare on high among the blest.
This body shall in silence sleep
Mine eyes no more shall ever weep
No fainting fits shall me assaile
nor grinding paines my body fraile
Wth cares and fears ne'r cumbred be
Nor losses know, nor sorrowes see
What tho my flesh shall there consume
it is the bed Christ did perfume

And when a few yeares shall be gone
this mortall shall be cloth'd vpon
A Corrupt Carcasse downe it lyes
a glorious body it shall rise
In weaknes and dishonour sowne
in power 'tis rais'd by Christ alone
Then soule and body shall vnite
and of their maker haue the sight
Such lasting ioyes shall there behold
as eare ne'r heard nor tongue e'er told
Lord make me ready for that day
then Come deare bridgrome Come away.

The Author To Her Book
Thou ill-form'd offspring of my feeble brain,
Who after birth did'st by my side remain,
Till snatcht from thence by friends, less wise than true,
Who thee abroad expos'd to public view,
Made thee in rags, halting to th' press to trudge,
Where errors were not lessened (all may judge).
At thy return my blushing was not small,
My rambling brat (in print) should mother call.
I cast thee by as one unfit for light,
Thy Visage was so irksome in my sight,
Yet being mine own, at length affection would
Thy blemishes amend, if so I could.
I wash'd thy face, but more defects I saw,
And rubbing off a spot, still made a flaw.
I stretcht thy joints to make thee even feet,
Yet still thou run'st more hobbling than is meet.
In better dress to trim thee was my mind,
But nought save home-spun Cloth, i' th' house I find.
In this array, 'mongst Vulgars mayst thou roam.
In Critics' hands, beware thou dost not come,
And take thy way where yet thou art not known.
If for thy Father askt, say, thou hadst none;
And for thy Mother, she alas is poor,
Which caus'd her thus to send thee out of door.

Before The Birth Of One Of Her Children
All things within this fading world hath end,
Adversity doth still our joys attend;
No ties so strong, no friends so dear and sweet,
But with death's parting blow are sure to meet.
The sentence past is most irrevocable,

A common thing, yet oh, inevitable.
How soon, my Dear, death may my steps attend,
How soon't may be thy lot to lose thy friend,
We both are ignorant, yet love bids me
These farewell lines to recommend to thee,
That when the knot's untied that made us one,
I may seem thine, who in effect am none.
And if I see not half my days that's due,
What nature would, God grant to yours and you;
The many faults that well you know I have
Let be interred in my oblivious grave;
If any worth or virtue were in me,
Let that live freshly in thy memory
And when thou feel'st no grief, as I no harmes,
Yet love thy dead, who long lay in thine arms,
And when thy loss shall be repaid with gains
Look to my little babes, my dear remains.
And if thou love thyself, or loved'st me,
These O protect from stepdame's injury.
And if chance to thine eyes shall bring this verse,
With some sad sighs honor my absent hearse;
And kiss this paper for thy dear love's sake,
Who with salt tears this last farewell did take.

By Night When Others Soundly Slept
By night when others soundly slept
And hath at once both ease and Rest,
My waking eyes were open kept
And so to lie I found it best.

I sought him whom my Soul did Love,
With tears I sought him earnestly.
He bow'd his ear down from Above.
In vain I did not seek or cry.

My hungry Soul he fill'd with Good;
He in his Bottle put my tears,
My smarting wounds washt in his blood,
And banisht thence my Doubts and fears.

What to my Saviour shall I give
Who freely hath done this for me?
I'll serve him here whilst I shall live
And Loue him to Eternity

Childhood

Ah me! conceiv'd in sin, and born in sorrow,
A nothing, here to day, but gone to morrow,
Whose mean beginning, blushing can't reveal,
But night and darkness must with shame conceal.
My mother's breeding sickness, I will spare,
Her nine months' weary burden not declare.
To shew her bearing pangs, I should do wrong,
To tell that pain, which can't be told by tongue.
With tears into this world I did arrive;
My mother still did waste, as I did thrive,
Who yet with love and all alacrity,
Spending was willing to be spent for me.
With wayward cries, I did disturb her rest,
Who sought still to appease me with her breast;
With weary arms, she danc'd, and By, By, sung,
When wretched I (ungrate) had done the wrong.
When Infancy was past, my Childishness
Did act all folly that it could express.
My silliness did only take delight
In that which riper age did scorn and slight,
In Rattles, Bables, and such toyish stuff.
My then ambitious thoughts were low enough.
My high-born soul so straitly was confin'd
That its own worth it did not know nor mind.
This little house of flesh did spacious count,
Through ignorance, all troubles did surmount,
Yet this advantage had mine ignorance,
Freedom from Envy and from Arrogance.
How to be rich, or great, I did not cark,
A Baron or a Duke ne'r made my mark,
Nor studious was, Kings favours how to buy,
With costly presents, or base flattery;
No office coveted, wherein I might
Make strong my self and turn aside weak right.
No malice bare to this or that great Peer,
Nor unto buzzing whisperers gave ear.
I gave no hand, nor vote, for death, or life.
I'd nought to do, 'twixt Prince, and peoples' strife.
No Statist I: nor Marti'list i' th' field.
Where e're I went, mine innocence was shield.
My quarrels, not for Diadems, did rise,
But for an Apple, Plumb, or some such prize.
My strokes did cause no death, nor wounds, nor scars.
My little wrath did cease soon as my wars.
My duel was no challenge, nor did seek.
My foe should weltering, with his bowels reek.

I had no Suits at law, neighbours to vex,
Nor evidence for land did me perplex.
I fear'd no storms, nor all the winds that blows.
I had no ships at Sea, no fraughts to loose.
I fear'd no drought, nor wet; I had no crop,
Nor yet on future things did place my hope.
This was mine innocence, but oh the seeds
Lay raked up of all the cursed weeds,
Which sprouted forth in my insuing age,
As he can tell, that next comes on the stage.
But let me yet relate, before I go,
The sins and dangers I am subject to:
From birth stained, with Adam's sinful fact,
From thence I 'gan to sin, as soon as act;
A perverse will, a love to what's forbid;
A serpent's sting in pleasing face lay hid;
A lying tongue as soon as it could speak
And fifth Commandment do daily break;
Oft stubborn, peevish, sullen, pout, and cry;
Then nought can please, and yet I know not why.
As many was my sins, so dangers too,
For sin brings sorrow, sickness, death, and woe,
And though I miss the tossings of the mind,
Yet griefs in my frail flesh I still do find.
What gripes of wind, mine infancy did pain?
What tortures I, in breeding teeth sustain?
What crudities my cold stomach hath bred?
Whence vomits, worms, and flux have issued?
What breaches, knocks, and falls I daily have?
And some perhaps, I carry to my grave.
Sometimes in fire, sometimes in water fall:
Strangely preserv'd, yet mind it not at all.
At home, abroad, my danger's manifold
That wonder 'tis, my glass till now doth hold.
I've done: unto my elders I give way,
For 'tis but little that a child can say.

Contemplations

Sometime now past in the Autumnal Tide,
When Ph{oe}bus wanted but one hour to bed,
The trees all richly clad, yet void of pride,
Were gilded o're by his rich golden head.
Their leaves and fruits seem'd painted but was true
Of green, of red, of yellow, mixed hew,
Rapt were my senses at this delectable view.

I wist not what to wish, yet sure thought I,
If so much excellence abide below,
How excellent is he that dwells on high?
Whose power and beauty by his works we know.
Sure he is goodness, wisdom, glory, light,
That hath this under world so richly dight.
More Heaven than Earth was here, no winter and no night.

Then on a stately Oak I cast mine Eye,
Whose ruffling top the Clouds seem'd to aspire.
How long since thou wast in thine Infancy?
Thy strength and stature, more thy years admire,
Hath hundred winters past since thou wast born?
Or thousand since thou brakest thy shell of horn?
If so, all these as nought, Eternity doth scorn.

Then higher on the glistering Sun I gaz'd,
Whose beams was shaded by the leafy Tree.
The more I look'd, the more I grew amaz'd
And softly said, what glory's like to thee?
Soul of this world, this Universe's Eye,
No wonder some made thee a Deity.
Had I not better known (alas) the same had I.

Thou as a Bridegroom from thy Chamber rushes
And as a strong man joys to run a race.
The morn doth usher thee with smiles and blushes.
The Earth reflects her glances in thy face.
Birds, insects, Animals with Vegative,
Thy heat from death and dullness doth revive
And in the darksome womb of fruitful nature dive.

Thy swift Annual and diurnal Course,
Thy daily straight and yearly oblique path,
Thy pleasing fervour, and thy scorching force,
All mortals here the feeling knowledge hath.
Thy presence makes it day, thy absence night,
Quaternal seasons caused by thy might.
Hail Creature, full of sweetness, beauty, and delight!

Art thou so full of glory that no Eye
Hath strength thy shining Rays once to behold?
And is thy splendid Throne erect so high
As, to approach it, can no earthly mould?
How full of glory then must thy Creator be!
Who gave this bright light luster unto thee.
Admir'd, ador'd for ever be that Majesty!

Silent alone where none or saw or heard,
In pathless paths I lead my wand'ring feet.
My humble Eyes to lofty Skies I rear'd
To sing some Song my mazed Muse thought meet.
My great Creator I would magnify
That nature had thus decked liberally,
But Ah and Ah again, my imbecility!

I heard the merry grasshopper then sing,
The black clad Cricket bear a second part.
They kept one tune and played on the same string,
Seeming to glory in their little Art.
Shall creatures abject thus their voices raise
And in their kind resound their maker's praise
Whilst I, as mute, can warble forth no higher lays?

When present times look back to Ages past
And men in being fancy those are dead,
It makes things gone perpetually to last
And calls back months and years that long since fled.
It makes a man more aged in conceit
Than was Methuselah or's grand-sire great,
While of their persons and their acts his mind doth treat.

Sometimes in Eden fair he seems to be,
See glorious Adam there made Lord of all,
Fancies the Apple dangle on the Tree
That turn'd his Sovereign to a naked thrall,
Who like a miscreant's driven from that place
To get his bread with pain and sweat of face.
A penalty impos'd on his backsliding Race.

Here sits our Grand-dame in retired place
And in her lap her bloody Cain new born.
The weeping Imp oft looks her in the face,
Bewails his unknown hap and fate forlorn.
His Mother sighs to think of Paradise
And how she lost her bliss to be more wise,
Believing him that was and is Father of lies.

Here Cain and Abel come to sacrifice,
Fruits of the Earth and Fatlings each do bring.
On Abel's gift the fire descends from Skies,
But no such sign on false Cain's offering.
With sullen hateful looks he goes his ways,
Hath thousand thoughts to end his brother's days,

Upon whose blood his future good he hopes to raise.

There Abel keeps his sheep, no ill he thinks,
His brother comes, then acts his fratricide.
The Virgin Earth of blood her first draught drinks,
But since that time she often hath been cloy'd.
The wretch with ghastly face and dreadful mind
Thinks each he sees will serve him in his kind,
Though none on Earth but kindred near then could he find.

Who fancies not his looks now at the Bar,
His face like death, his heart with horror fraught.
Nor Male-factor ever felt like war,
When deep despair with wish of life hath fought,
Branded with guilt, and crusht with treble woes,
A Vagabond to Land of Nod he goes,
A City builds that walls might him secure from foes.

Who thinks not oft upon the Father's ages?
Their long descent, how nephews' sons they saw,
The starry observations of those Sages,
And how their precepts to their sons were law,
How Adam sigh'd to see his Progeny
Cloth'd all in his black, sinful Livery,
Who neither guilt not yet the punishment could fly.

Our life compare we with their length of days.
Who to the tenth of theirs doth now arrive?
And though thus short, we shorten many ways,
Living so little while we are alive.
In eating, drinking, sleeping, vain delight
So unawares comes on perpetual night
And puts all pleasures vain unto eternal flight.

When I behold the heavens as in their prime
And then the earth (though old) still clad in green,
The stones and trees, insensible of time,
Nor age nor wrinkle on their front are seen.
If winter come and greenness then do fade,
A Spring returns, and they more youthful made,
But Man grows old, lies down, remains where once he's laid.

By birth more noble than those creatures all,
Yet seems by nature and by custom curs'd,
No sooner born but grief and care makes fall
That state obliterate he had at first:
Nor youth, nor strength, nor wisdom spring again,

Nor habitations long their names retain
But in oblivion to the final day remain.

Shall I then praise the heavens, the trees, the earth,
Because their beauty and their strength last longer?
Shall I wish there, or never to had birth,
Because they're bigger and their bodies stronger?
Nay, they shall darken, perish, fade and die,
And when unmade, so ever shall they lie.
But man was made for endless immortality.

Under the cooling shadow of a stately Elm
Close sate I by a goodly River's side,
Where gliding streams the Rocks did overwhelm.
A lonely place, with pleasures dignifi'd.
I once that lov'd the shady woods so well,
Now thought the rivers did the trees excel,
And if the sun would ever shine, there would I dwell.

While on the stealing stream I fixt mine eye,
Which to the long'd-for Ocean held its course,
I markt nor crooks, nor rubs that there did lie
Could hinder ought but still augment its force.
O happy Flood, quoth I, that holds thy race
Till thou arrive at thy beloved place,
Nor is it rocks or shoals that can obstruct thy pace.

Nor is't enough that thou alone may'st slide,
But hundred brooks in thy clear waves do meet,
So hand in hand along with thee they glide
To Thetis' house, where all imbrace and greet.
Thou Emblem true of what I count the best,
O could I lead my Rivolets to rest,
So may we press to that vast mansion, ever blest.

Ye Fish which in this liquid Region 'bide
That for each season have your habitation,
Now salt, now fresh where you think best to glide
To unknown coasts to give a visitation,
In Lakes and ponds, you leave your numerous fry.
So Nature taught, and yet you know not why,
You watry folk that know not your felicity.

Look how the wantons frisk to task the air,
Then to the colder bottom straight they dive;
Eftsoon to Neptune's glassy Hall repair
To see what trade they, great ones, there do drive,

Who forrage o're the spacious sea-green field
And take the trembling prey before it yield,
Whose armour is their scales, their spreading fins their shield.

While musing thus with contemplation fed,
And thousand fancies buzzing in my brain,
The sweet-tongu'd Philomel percht o're my head
And chanted forth a most melodious strain
Which rapt me so with wonder and delight
I judg's my hearing better than my sight
And wisht me wings with her a while to take my flight.

O merry Bird (said I) that fears no snares,
That neither toils nor hoards up in thy barn,
Feels no sad thoughts nor cruciating cares
To gain more good or shun what might thee harm
Thy clothes ne'er wear, thy meat is everywhere,
Thy bed a bough, thy drink the water clear
Reminds not what is past, nor what's to come dost fear.

The dawning morn with songs thou dost prevent,
Sets hundred notes unto thy feathered crew,
So each one tunes his pretty instrument
And warbling out the old, begin anew,
And thus they pass their youth in summer season,
Then follow thee into a better Region,
Where winter's never felt by that sweet airy legion.

Man at the best a creature frail and vain,
In knowledge ignorant, in strength but weak,
Subject to sorrows, losses, sickness, pain,
Each storm his state, his mind, his body break
From some of these he never finds cessation
But day or night, within, without, vexation,
Troubles from foes, from friends, from dearest, near'st Relation.

And yet this sinful creature, frail and vain,
This lump of wretchedness, of sin and sorrow,
This weather-beaten vessel wrackt with pain,
Joys not in hope of an eternal morrow.
Nor all his losses, crosses, and vexation,
In weight, in frequency and long duration
Can make him deeply groan for that divine Translation.

The Mariner that on smooth waves doth glide
Sings merrily and steers his Barque with ease
As if he had command of wind and tide

And now becomes great Master of the seas,
But suddenly a storm spoils all the sport
And makes him long for a more quiet port,
Which 'gainst all adverse winds may serve for fort.

So he that faileth in this world of pleasure,
Feeding on sweets that never bit of th' sour,
That's full of friends, of honour, and of treasure,
Fond fool, he takes this earth ev'n for heav'ns bower,
But sad affliction comes and makes him see
Here's neither honour, wealth, or safety.
Only above is found all with security.

O Time the fatal wrack of mortal things
That draws oblivion's curtains over kings,
Their sumptuous monuments, men know them not;
Their names with a Record are forgot,
Their parts, their ports, their pomp's all laid in th' dust.
Nor wit, nor gold, nor buildings scape time's rust,
But he whose name is grav'd in the white stone
Shall last and shine when all of these are gone.

To My Dear Children
This Book by Any yet vnread,
I leaue for yov when I am dead,
That, being gone, here yov may find
What was your liueing mother's mind.
Make vse of what I leaue in Loue
And God shall blesse yov from above.

To My Dear And Loving Husband
If ever two were one, then surely we.
If ever man were lov'd by wife, then thee.
If ever wife was happy in a man,
Compare with me, ye women, if you can.
I prize thy love more than whole Mines of gold
Or all the riches that the East doth hold.
My love is such that Rivers cannot quench,
Nor ought but love from thee give recompetence.
Thy love is such I can no way repay.
The heavens reward thee manifold, I pray.
Then while we live, in love let's so persever
That when we live no more, we may live ever.

David's Lamentation for Saul and Jonathan

Alas slain is the Head of Israel,
Illustrious Saul whose beauty did excell,
Upon thy places mountainous and high,
How did the Mighty fall, and falling dye?
In Gath let not this things be spoken on,
Nor published in streets of Askalon,
Lest daughters of the Philistines rejoyce,
Lest the uncircumcis'd lift up their voice.
O Gilbo Mounts, let never pearled dew,
Nor fruitfull showres your barren tops bestrew,
Nor fields of offrings ever on you grow,
Nor any pleasant thing e're may you show;
For there the Mighty Ones did soon decay,
The shield of Saul was vilely cast away,
There had his dignity so sore a foyle,
As if his head ne're felt the sacred oyle.
Sometimes from crimson, blood of gastly slain,
The bow of Jonathan ne're turn'd in vain:
Nor from the fat, and spoils of Mighty men
With bloodless sword did Saul turn back agen.
Pleasant and lovely, were they both in life,
And in their death was found no parting strife.
Swifter then swiftest Eagles so were they,
Stronger then Lions ramping for their prey.
O Israels Dames, o'reflow your beauteous eyes
For valiant Saul who on Mount Gilbo lyes,
Who cloathed you in Cloath of richest Dye,
And choice delights, full of variety,
On your array put ornaments of gold,
Which made you yet more beauteous to behold.
O! how in Battle did the mighty fall
In midst of strength not succoured at all.
O lovely Jonathan! how wast thou slain?
In places high, full low thou didst remain.
Distrest for thee I am, dear Jonathan,
Thy love was wonderfull, surpassing man,
Exceeding all the love that's Feminine,
So pleasant hast thou been, dear brother mine,
How are the mighty fall'n into decay?
And warlike weapons perished away?

Deliverance From A Fit Of Fainting
Worthy art Thou, O Lord, of praise,
But ah! It's not in me.
My sinking heart I pray Thee raise
So shall I give it Thee.

My life as spider's webb's cut off,
Thus fainting have I said,
And living man no more shall see
But be in silence laid.

My feeble spirit Thou didst revive,
My doubting Thou didst chide,
And though as dead mad'st me alive,
I here a while might 'bide.

Why should I live but to Thy praise?
My life is hid with Thee.
O Lord, no longer be my days
Than I may fruitful be.

Deliverance From Another Sore Fit
In my distress I sought the Lord
When naught on earth could comfort give,
And when my soul these things abhorred,
Then, Lord, Thou said'st unto me, "Live."

Thou knowest the sorrows that I felt;
My plaints and groans were heard of Thee,
And how in sweat I seemed to melt
Thou help'st and Thou regardest me.

My wasted flesh Thou didst restore,
My feeble loins didst gird with strength,
Yea, when I was most low and poor,
I said I shall praise Thee at length.

What shall I render to my God
For all His bounty showed to me?
Even for His mercies in His rod,
Where pity most of all I see.

My heart I wholly give to Thee;
O make it fruitful, faithful Lord.
My life shall dedicated be
To praise in thought, in deed, in word.

Thou know'st no life I did require
Longer than still Thy name to praise,
Nor ought on earth worthy desire,
In drawing out these wretched days.

Thy name and praise to celebrate,
O Lord, for aye is my request.
O grant I do it in this state,
And then with Thee, which is the best.

Her Mother's Epitaph
Here lies
A worthy matron of unspotted life,
A loving mother and obedient wife,
A friendly neighbor, pitiful to poor,
Whom oft she fed, and clothed with her store;
To servants wisely aweful, but yet kind,
And as they did, so they reward did find:
A true instructor of her family,
The which she ordered with dexterity,
The public meetings ever did frequent,
And in her closest constant hours she spent;
Religious in all her words and ways,
Preparing still for death, till end of days:
Of all her children, children lived to see,
Then dying, left a blessed memory.

Her Father's Epitaph
Within this tomb a patriot lies
That was both pious, just and wise,
To truth a shield, to right a wall,
To sectaries a whip and maul,
A magazine of history,
A prizer of good company
In manners pleasant and severe
The good him loved, the bad did fear,
And when his time with years was spent
In some rejoiced, more did lament.
1653, age 77

In secret place where once I stood
Close by the Banks of Lacrim flood,
I heard two sisters reason on
Things that are past and things to come.
One Flesh was call'd, who had her eye
On worldly wealth and vanity;
The other Spirit, who did rear

Her thoughts unto a higher sphere.
"Sister," quoth Flesh, "what liv'st thou on
Nothing but Meditation?
Doth Contemplation feed thee so
Regardlessly to let earth go?
Can Speculation satisfy
Notion without Reality?
Dost dream of things beyond the Moon
And dost thou hope to dwell there soon?
Hast treasures there laid up in store
That all in th' world thou count'st but poor?
Art fancy-sick or turn'd a Sot
To catch at shadows which are not?
Come, come. I'll show unto thy sense,
Industry hath its recompence.
What canst desire, but thou maist see
True substance in variety?
Dost honour like? Acquire the same,
As some to their immortal fame;
And trophies to thy name erect
Which wearing time shall ne'er deject.
For riches dost thou long full sore?
Behold enough of precious store.
Earth hath more silver, pearls, and gold
Than eyes can see or hands can hold.
Affects thou pleasure? Take thy fill.
Earth hath enough of what you will.
Then let not go what thou maist find
For things unknown only in mind."

For Deliverance From A Feaver
When Sorrowes had begyrt me rovnd,
And Paines within and out,
When in my flesh no part was sovnd,
Then didst thou rid me out.
My burning flesh in sweat did boyle,
My aking head did break;
From side to side for ease I toyle,
So faint I could not speak.
Beclouded was my Soul with fear
Of thy Displeasure sore,
Nor could I read my Evidence
Which oft I read before.
Hide not thy face from me, I cry'd,
From Burnings keep my soul;
Thov know'st my heart, and hast me try'd;

I on thy Mercyes Rowl.
O, heal my Soul, thov know'st I said,
Tho' flesh consume to novght;
What tho' in dust it shall bee lay'd,
To Glory't shall bee brovght.
Thou heardst, thy rod thou didst remove,
And spar'd my Body frail,
Thou shew'st to me thy tender Love,
My heart no more might quail.
O, Praises to my mighty God,
Praise to my Lord, I say,
Who hath redeem'd my Soul from pitt:
Praises to him for Aye!

Upon My Daughter Hannah Wiggin Her Recouery From A Dangerous Feaver

Bles't bee thy Name, who did'st restore
To health my Daughter dear
When death did seem ev'n to approach,
And life was ended near.
Gravnt shee remember what thov'st done,
And celebrate thy Praise;
And let her Conversation say,
Shee loues thee all thy Dayes.

Upon a Fit of Sickness, Anno 1632 Aetatis Suae, 19

Twice ten years old not fully told
since nature gave me breath,
My race is run, my thread spun,
lo, here is fatal death.
All men must die, and so must I;
this cannot be revoked.
For Adam's sake this word God spake
when he so high provoked.
Yet live I shall, this life's but small,
in place of highest bliss,
Where I shall have all I can crave,
no life is like to this.
For what's this but care and strife
since first we came from womb?
Our strength doth waste, our time doth haste,
and then we go to th' tomb.
O bubble blast, how long can'st last?
that always art a breaking,
No sooner blown, but dead and gone,

ev'n as a word that's speaking.
O whilst I live this grace me give,
I doing good may be,
Then death's arrest I shall count best,
because it's Thy decree;
Bestow much cost there's nothing lost,
to make salvation sure,
O great's the gain, though got with pain,
comes by profession pure.
The race is run, the field is won,
the victory's mine I see;
Forever known, thou envious foe,
the foil belongs to thee.

For The Restoration Of My Dear Husband From A Burning Ague, June, 1661

When feares and sorrowes me besett,
Then did'st thou rid me out;
When heart did faint and spirits quail,
Thou comforts me about.
Thou rais'st him vp I feard to loose,
Regau'st me him again:
Distempers thou didst chase away;
With strenght didst him sustain.
My thankfull heart, with Pen record
The Goodnes of thy God;
Let thy obedience testefye
He taught thee by his rod.
And with his staffe did thee support,
That thou by both may'st learn;
And 'twixt the good and evill way,
At last, thou mig'st discern.
Praises to him who hath not left
My Soul as destitute;
Nor turnd his ear away from me,
But graunted hath my Suit.

Here Follow Several Occasional Meditations

By night when others soundly slept,
And had at once both case and rest,
My waking eyes were open kept
And so to lie I found it best.

I sought Him whom my soul did love,
With tears I sought Him earnestly;

He bowed His ear down from above.
In vain I did not seek or cry.

My hungry soul He filled with good,
He in His bottle put my tears,
My smarting wounds washed in His blood,
And banished thence my doubts and fears.

What to my Savior shall I give,
Who freely hath done this for me?
I'll serve Him here whilst I shall live
And love Him to eternity.

Here Follows Some Verses Upon The Burning Of Our House, July 18th, 1666

In silent night when rest I took
For sorrow near I did not look
I waked was with thund'ring noise
And piteous shrieks of dreadful voice.
That fearful sound of "Fire!" and "Fire!"
Let no man know is my desire.
I, starting up, the light did spy,
And to my God my heart did cry
To strengthen me in my distress
And not to leave me succorless.
Then, coming out, beheld a space
The flame consume my dwelling place.
And when I could no longer look,
I blest His name that gave and took,
That laid my goods now in the dust.
Yea, so it was, and so 'twas just.
It was His own, it was not mine,
Far be it that I should repine;
He might of all justly bereft
But yet sufficient for us left.
When by the ruins oft I past
My sorrowing eyes aside did cast,
And here and there the places spy
Where oft I sat and long did lie:
Here stood that trunk, and there that chest,
There lay that store I counted best.
My pleasant things in ashes lie,
And them behold no more shall I.
Under thy roof no guest shall sit,
Nor at thy table eat a bit.
No pleasant tale shall e'er be told,

Nor things recounted done of old.
No candle e'er shall shine in thee,
Nor bridegroom's voice e'er heard shall be.
In silence ever shall thou lie,
Adieu, Adieu, all's vanity.
Then straight I 'gin my heart to chide,
And did thy wealth on earth abide?
Didst fix thy hope on mold'ring dust?
The arm of flesh didst make thy trust?
Raise up thy thoughts above the sky
That dunghill mists away may fly.
Thou hast an house on high erect,
Framed by that mighty Architect,
With glory richly furnished,
Stands permanent though this be fled.
It's purchased and paid for too
By Him who hath enough to do.
A price so vast as is unknown
Yet by His gift is made thine own;
There's wealth enough, I need no more,
Farewell, my pelf, farewell my store.
The world no longer let me love,
My hope and treasure lies above.

In Honour Of That High And Mighty Princess, Queen Elizabeth Proem

Although great Queen, thou now in silence lie,
Yet thy loud Herald Fame, doth to the sky
Thy wondrous worth proclaim, in every clime,
And so has vow'd, whilst there is world or time.
So great's thy glory, and thine excellence,
The sound thereof raps every human sense
That men account it no impiety
To say thou wert a fleshly Deity.
Thousands bring off'rings (though out of date)
Thy world of honours to accumulate.
'Mongst hundred Hecatombs of roaring Verse,
'Mine bleating stands before thy royal Hearse.
Thou never didst, nor canst thou now disdain,
T' accept the tribute of a loyal Brain.
Thy clemency did yerst esteem as much
The acclamations of the poor, as rich,
Which makes me deem, my rudeness is no wrong,
Though I resound thy greatness 'mongst the throng.

The Poem.

No Ph{oe}nix Pen, nor Spenser's Poetry,
No Speed's, nor Camden's learned History;
Eliza's works, wars, praise, can e're compact,
The World's the Theater where she did act.
No memories, nor volumes can contain,
The nine Olymp'ades of her happy reign,
Who was so good, so just, so learn'd, so wise,
From all the Kings on earth she won the prize.
or say I more than truly is her due.
Millions will testify that this is true.
She hath wip'd off th' aspersion of her Sex,
That women wisdom lack to play the Rex.
Spain's Monarch sa's not so, not yet his Host:
She taught them better manners to their cost.
The Salic Law had not in force now been,
If France had ever hop'd for such a Queen.
But can you Doctors now this point dispute,
She's argument enough to make you mute,
Since first the Sun did run, his ne'er runn'd race,
And earth had twice a year, a new old face;
Since time was time, and man unmanly man,
Come shew me such a Ph{oe}nix if you can.
Was ever people better rul'd than hers?
Was ever Land more happy, freed from stirs?
Did ever wealth in England so abound?
Her Victories in foreign Coasts resound?
Ships more invincible than Spain's, her foe
She rack't, she sack'd, she sunk his Armadoe.
Her stately Troops advanc'd to Lisbon's wall,
Don Anthony in's right for to install.
She frankly help'd Franks' (brave) distressed King,
The States united now her fame do sing.
She their Protectrix was, they well do know,
Unto our dread Virago, what they owe.
Her Nobles sacrific'd their noble blood,
Nor men, nor coin she shap'd, to do them good.
The rude untamed Irish she did quell,
And Tiron bound, before her picture fell.
Had ever Prince such Counsellors as she?
Her self Minerva caus'd them so to be.
Such Soldiers, and such Captains never seen,
As were the subjects of our (Pallas) Queen:
Her Sea-men through all straits the world did round,
Terra incognitæ might know her sound.
Her Drake came laded home with Spanish gold,
Her Essex took Cadiz, their Herculean hold.
But time would fail me, so my wit would too,

To tell of half she did, or she could do.
Semiramis to her is but obscure;
More infamy than fame she did procure.
She plac'd her glory but on Babel's walls,
World's wonder for a time, but yet it falls.
Fierce Tomris (Cirus' Heads-man, Sythians' Queen)
Had put her Harness off, had she but seen
Our Amazon i' th' Camp at Tilbury,
(Judging all valour, and all Majesty)
Within that Princess to have residence,
And prostrate yielded to her Excellence.
Dido first Foundress of proud Carthage walls
(Who living consummates her Funerals),
A great Eliza, but compar'd with ours,
How vanisheth her glory, wealth, and powers.
Proud profuse Cleopatra, whose wrong name,
Instead of glory, prov'd her Country's shame:
Of her what worth in Story's to be seen,
But that she was a rich Ægyptian Queen.
Zenobia, potent Empress of the East,
And of all these without compare the best
(Whom none but great Aurelius could quell)
Yet for our Queen is no fit parallel:
She was a Ph{oe}nix Queen, so shall she be,
Her ashes not reviv'd more Ph{oe}nix she.
Her personal perfections, who would tell,
Must dip his Pen i' th' Heliconian Well,
Which I may not, my pride doth but aspire
To read what others write and then admire.
Now say, have women worth, or have they none?
Or had they some, but with our Queen is't gone?
Nay Masculines, you have thus tax'd us long,
But she, though dead, will vindicate our wrong.
Let such as say our sex is void of reason
Know 'tis a slander now, but once was treason.
But happy England, which had such a Queen,
O happy, happy, had those days still been,
But happiness lies in a higher sphere.
Then wonder not, Eliza moves not here.
Full fraught with honour, riches, and with days,
She set, she set, like Titan in his rays.
No more shall rise or set such glorious Sun,
Until the heaven's great revolution:
If then new things, their old form must retain,
Eliza shall rule Albian once again.

Her Epitaph.

Here sleeps T H E Queen, this is the royal bed
O' th' Damask Rose, sprung from the white and red,
Whose sweet perfume fills the all-filling air,
This Rose is withered, once so lovely fair:
On neither tree did grow such Rose before,
The greater was our gain, our loss the more.

Another.
Here lies the pride of Queens, pattern of Kings:
So blaze it fame, here's feathers for thy wings.
Here lies the envy'd, yet unparallel'd Prince,
Whose living virtues speak (though dead long since).
If many worlds, as that fantastic framed,
In every one, be her great glory famed

Upon My Son Samuel His Goeing For England, November 6, 1657

Thou mighty God of Sea and Land,
I here resigne into thy hand
The Son of Prayers, of vowes, of teares,
The child I stay'd for many yeares.
Thou heard'st me then, and gav'st him me;
Hear me again, I giue him Thee.
He's mine, but more, O Lord, thine own,
For sure thy Grace on him is shown.
No freind I haue like Thee to trust,
For mortall helpes are brittle Dvst.
Preserve, O Lord, from stormes and wrack,
Protect him there, and bring him back;
And if thou shalt spare me a space,
That I again may see his face,
Then shall I celebrate thy Praise,
And Blesse the for't even all my Dayes.
If otherwise I goe to Rest,
Thy Will bee done, for that is best;
Perswade my heart I shall him see
For ever happefy'd with Thee.

Upon My Dear and Loving Husband His Going Into England January 16, 1661

O thou Most High who rulest all
And hear'st the prayers of thine,
O hearken, Lord, unto my suit
And my petition sign.

Into Thy everlasting arms Of mercy
I commend Thy servant, Lord.
Keep and preserve My husband,
my dear friend.

At Thy command, O Lord, he went,
Nor nought could keep him back.
Then let Thy promise joy his heart,
O help and be not slack.

Uphold my heart in Thee, O God.
Thou art my strength and stay,
Thou see'st how weak and frail I am,
Hide not Thy face away.

I in obedience to Thy will
Thou knowest did submit.
It was my duty so to do;
O Lord, accept of it.

Unthankfulness for mercies past
Impute Thou not to me.
O Lord, Thou know'st my weak desire
Was to sing praise to Thee.

Lord, be Thou pilot to the ship
And send them prosperous gales.
In storms and sickness, Lord, preserve.
Thy goodness never fails.

Unto Thy work he hath in hand
Lord, grant Thou good success
And favour in their eyes to whom
He shall make his address.

Remember, Lord, Thy folk whom Thou
To wilderness hast brought;
Let not Thine own inheritance
Be sold away for nought.

But tokens of Thy favour give,
With joy send back my dear
That I and all Thy servants may
Rejoice with heavenly cheer.

Lord, let my eyes see once again
Him whom Thou gavest me

That we together may sing praise
Forever unto Thee.

And the remainder of our days
Shall consecrated be
With an engaged heart to sing
All praises unto Thee.

In My Solitary Hours In My Dear Husband His Absence
O Lord, Thou hear'st my daily moan
And see'st my dropping tears.
My troubles all are Thee before,
My longings and my fears.

Thou hitherto hast been my God;
Thy help my soul hath found.
Though loss and sickness me assailed,
Through Thee I've kept my ground.

And Thy abode Thou'st made with me;
With Thee my soul can talk;
In secret places Thee I find
Where I do kneel or walk.

Though husband dear be from me gone,
Whom I do love so well,
I have a more beloved one
Whose comforts far excel.

O stay my heart on Thee. my God,
Uphold my fainting soul.
And when I know not what to do,
I'll on Thy mercies roll.

My weakness. Thou dost know full well
Of body and of mind;
I in this world no comfort have,
But what from Thee I find.

Though children Thou has given me,
And friends I have also,
Yet if I see Thee not through them
They are no joy, but woe.

O shine upon me, blessed Lord,
Ev'n for my Saviour's sake;

In Thee alone is more than all,
And there content I'll take.

O hear me, Lord, in this request
As Thou before hast done,
Bring back my husband, I beseech,
As Thou didst once my son.

So shall I celebrate Thy praise
Ev'n while my days shall last
And talk to my beloved one
Of all Thy goodness past.

So both of us Thy kindness, Lord,
With praises shall recount
And serve Thee better than before
Whose blessings thus surmount.

But give me, Lord, a better heart,
Then better shall I be,
To pay the vows which I do owe
Forever unto Thee.

Unless Thou help, what can I do
But still my frailty show?
If Thou assist me, Lord,
I shall Return Thee what I owe.

In Reference To Her Children
I had eight birds hatched in one nest,
Four cocks there were, and hens the rest.
I nursed them up with pain and care,
Nor cost, nor labour did I spare,
Till at the last they felt their wing,
Mounted the trees, and learned to sing;
Chief of the brood then took his flight
To regions far and left me quite.
My mournful chirps I after send,
Till he return, or I do end:
Leave not thy nest, thy dam and sire,
Fly back and sing amidst this choir.
My second bird did take her flight,
And with her mate flew out of sight;
Southward they both their course did bend,
And seasons twain they there did spend,
Till after blown by southern gales,

They norward steered with filled sails.
A prettier bird was no where seen,
Along the beach among the treen.
I have a third of colour white,
On whom I placed no small delight;
Coupled with mate loving and true,
Hath also bid her dam adieu;
And where Aurora first appears,
She now hath perched to spend her years.
One to the academy flew
To chat among that learned crew;
Ambition moves still in his breast
That he might chant above the rest
Striving for more than to do well,
That nightingales he might excel.
My fifth, whose down is yet scarce gone,
Is 'mongst the shrubs and bushes flown,
And as his wings increase in strength,
On higher boughs he'll perch at length.
My other three still with me nest,
Until they're grown, then as the rest,
Or here or there they'll take their flight,
As is ordained, so shall they light.
If birds could weep, then would my tears
Let others know what are my fears
Lest this my brood some harm should catch,
And be surprised for want of watch,
Whilst pecking corn and void of care,
They fall un'wares in fowler's snare,
Or whilst on trees they sit and sing,
Some untoward boy at them do fling,
Or whilst allured with bell and glass,
The net be spread, and caught, alas.
Or lest by lime-twigs they be foiled,
Or by some greedy hawks be spoiled.
O would my young, ye saw my breast,
And knew what thoughts there sadly rest,
Great was my pain when I you fed,
Long did I keep you soft and warm,
And with my wings kept off all harm,
My cares are more and fears than ever,
My throbs such now as 'fore were never.
Alas, my birds, you wisdom want,
Of perils you are ignorant;
Oft times in grass, on trees, in flight,
Sore accidents on you may light.
O to your safety have an eye,

So happy may you live and die.
Meanwhile my days in tunes I'll spend,
Till my weak lays with me shall end.
In shady woods I'll sit and sing,
And things that past to mind I'll bring.
Once young and pleasant, as are you,
But former toys (no joys) adieu.
My age I will not once lament,
But sing, my time so near is spent.
And from the top bough take my flight
Into a country beyond sight,
Where old ones instantly grow young,
And there with seraphims set song;
No seasons cold, nor storms they see;
But spring lasts to eternity.
When each of you shall in your nest
Among your young ones take your rest,
In chirping language, oft them tell,
You had a dam that loved you well,
That did what could be done for young,
And nursed you up till you were strong,
And 'fore she once would let you fly,
She showed you joy and misery;
Taught what was good, and what was ill,
What would save life, and what would kill.
Thus gone, amongst you I may live,
And dead, yet speak, and counsel give:
Farewell, my birds, farewell adieu,
I happy am, if well with you.

In Thankful Remembrance For My Dear Husband's Safe Arrival September 3, 1662

What shall I render to Thy name
Or how Thy praises speak?
My thanks how shall I testify?
O Lord, Thou know'st I'm weak.

I owe so much, so little can
Return unto Thy name,
Confusion seizes on my soul,
And I am filled with shame.

O Thou that hearest prayers, Lord,
To Thee shall come all flesh
Thou hast me heard and answered,
My plaints have had access.

What did I ask for but Thou gav'st?
What could I more desire?
But thankfulness even all my days
I humbly this require.

Thy mercies, Lord, have been so great
In number numberless,
Impossible for to recount
Or any way express.

O help Thy saints that sought Thy face
T' return unto Thee praise
And walk before Thee as they ought,
In strict and upright ways.

Meditations Divine And Moral

A ship that bears much sail, and little ballast, is easily
overset; and that man, whose head hath great abilities, and his
heart little or no grace, is in danger of foundering.
The finest bread has the least bran; the purest honey, the
least wax; and the sincerest Christian, the least self-love.
Sweet words are like honey; a little may refresh, but too much
gluts the stomach.
Divers children have their different natures: some are like
flesh which nothing but salt will keep from putrefaction; some
again like tender fruits that are best preserved with sugar. Those
parents are wise that can fit their nurture according to their nature.
Authority without wisdom is like a heavy axe without an edge,
fitter to bruise than polish.
The reason why Christians are so loath to exchange this world
for a better, is because they have more sense than faith: they see
what they enjoy, they do but hope for that which is to come.
Dim eyes are the concomitants of old age; and short-
sightedness, in those that are the eyes of a Republic, foretells a
declining State.
Wickedness comes to its height by degrees. He that dares say
of a less sin, Is it not a little one? will erelong say of a
greater, Tush, God regards it not.
Fire hath its force abated by water, not by wind; and anger
must be allayed by cold words and not by blustering threats.
The gifts that God bestows on the sons of men, are not only
abused, but most commonly employed for a clean contrary end than
that which they were given for; as health, wealth, and honor, which
might be so many steps to draw men to God in consideration of his
bounty towards them, but have driven them the further from him,

that they are ready to say, We are lords, we will come no more at thee. If outward blessings be not as wings to help us mount upwards, they will certainly prove clogs and weights that will pull

My Thankfull Heart With Glorying Tongue

My thankfull heart with glorying Tongue
Shall celebrate thy Name,
Who hath restor'd, redeem'd, recur'd
From sicknes, death, and Pain.
I cry'd thov seem'st to make some stay,
I sovght more earnestly;
And in due time thou succóur'st me,
And sent'st me help from High.
Lord, whilst my fleeting time shall last,
Thy Goodnes let me Tell.
And new Experience I haue gain'd,
My future Doubts repell.
An humble, faitefull life, O Lord,
For ever let me walk;
Let my obedience testefye,
My Praise lyes not in Talk.
Accept, O Lord, my simple mite,
For more I cannot giue;
What thou bestow'st I shall restore,
For of thine Almes I liue.

To The Memory Of My Dear Daughter In Law, Mrs. Mercy Bradstreet, Who Deceased September 6 1669

And live I still to see Relations gone,
And yet survive to sound this wailing tone;
Ah, woe is me, to write thy Funeral Song,
Who might in reason yet have lived long,
I saw the branches lopt the Tree now fall,
I stood so nigh, it crusht me down withal;
My bruised heart lies sobbing at the Root,
That thou dear Son hath lost both Tree and fruit:
Thou then on Seas sailing to forreign Coast;
Was ignorant what riches thou hadst lost.
But ah too soon those heavy tydings fly,
To strike thee with amazing misery;
Oh how I simpathize with thy sad heart,
And in thy griefs still bear a second part:
I lost a daughter dear, but thou a wife,
Who lov'd thee more (it seem'd) then her own life.
Thou being gone, she longer could not be,

Because her Soul she'd sent along with thee.
One week she only past in pain and woe,
And then her sorrows all at once did go;
A Babe she left before, she soar'd above,
The fifth and last pledg of her dying love,
E're nature would, it hither did arrive,
No wonder it no longer did survive.
So with her Children four, she's now a rest,
All freed from grief (I trust) among the blest;
She one hath left, a joy to thee and me,
The Heavens vouchsafe she may so ever be.
Chear up, (dear Son) thy fainting bleeding heart,
In him alone, that caused all this smart;
What though thy strokes full sad & grievous be,
He knows it is the best for thee and me.

The Vanity Of All Worldly Things
As he said vanity, so vain say I,
Oh! Vanity, O vain all under sky;
Where is the man can say, "Lo, I have found
On brittle earth a consolation sound"?
What isn't in honor to be set on high?
No, they like beasts and sons of men shall die,
And whilst they live, how oft doth turn their fate;
He's now a captive that was king of late.
What isn't in wealth great treasures to obtain?
No, that's but labor, anxious care, and pain.
He heaps up riches, and he heaps up sorrow,
It's his today, but who's his heir tomorrow?
What then? Content in pleasures canst thou find?
More vain than all, that's but to grasp the wind.
The sensual senses for a time they pleasure,
Meanwhile the conscience rage, who shall appease?
What isn't in beauty? No that's but a snare,
They're foul enough today, that once were fair.
What is't in flow'ring youth, or manly age?
The first is prone to vice, the last to rage.
Where is it then, in wisdom, learning, arts?
Sure if on earth, it must be in those parts;
Yet these the wisest man of men did find
But vanity, vexation of the mind.
And he that know the most doth still bemoan
He knows not all that here is to be known.
What is it then? To do as stoics tell,
Nor laugh, nor weep, let things go ill or well?
Such stoics are but stocks, such teaching vain,

While man is man, he shall have ease or pain.
If not in honor, beauty, age, nor treasure,
Nor yet in learning, wisdom, youth, nor pleasure,
Where shall I climb, sound, seek, search, or find
That summum bonum which may stay my mind?
There is a path no vulture's eye hath seen,
Where lion fierce, nor lion's whelps have been,
Which leads unto that living crystal fount,
Who drinks thereof, the world doth naught account.
The depth and sea have said " 'tis not in me,"
With pearl and gold it shall not valued be.
For sapphire, onyx, topaz who would change;
It's hid from eyes of men, they count it strange.
Death and destruction the fame hath heard,
But where and what it is, from heaven's declared;
It brings to honor which shall ne'er decay,
It stores with wealth which time can't wear away.
It yieldeth pleasures far beyond conceit,
And truly beautifies without deceit.
Nor strength, nor wisdom, nor fresh youth shall fade,
Nor death shall see, but are immortal made.
This pearl of price, this tree of life, this spring,
Who is possessed of shall reign a king.
Nor change of state nor cares shall ever see,
But wear his crown unto eternity.
This satiates the soul, this stays the mind,
And all the rest, but vanity we find.

On My Son's Return Out Of England, July 17, 1661.
All Praise to him who hath now turn'd
My feares to Joyes, my sighes to song,
My Teares to smiles, my sad to glad:
He's come for whom I waited long.
Thou di'st preserve him as he went;
In raging stormes did'st safely keep:
Did'st that ship bring to quiet Port.
The other sank low in the Deep.
From Dangers great thou did'st him free
Of Pyrates who were neer at hand;
And order'st so the adverse wind,
That he before them gott to Land.
In covntry strange thou did'st provide
And freinds rais'd him in euery Place;
And courtesies of svndry sorts
From such as 'fore nere saw his face.
In sicknes when he lay full sore,

His help and his Physitian wer't;
When royall ones that Time did dye,
Thou heal'dst his flesh, and cheer'd his heart.
From troubles and Incúbers Thov,
Without (all fraud), did'st sett him free,
That, without scandall, he might come
To th'Land of his Nativity.
On Eagles wings him hether brovght
Thro: Want and Dangers manifold;
And thvs hath gravnted my Reqvest,
That I thy Mercyes might behold.
O help me pay my Vowes, O Lord!
That ever I may thankfull bee,
And may putt him in mind of what
Tho'st done for him, and so for me.
In both our hearts erect a frame
Of Duty and of Thankfullnes,
That all thy favours great receiv'd,
Oure vpright walking may expresse.
O Lord, gravnt that I may never forgett thy
Loving kindnes in this Particular,
and how gratiovsly thov hast answered my Desires.

On My Dear Grand-Child Simon Bradstreet, Who Dyed On 16 November 1669 Being But A Moneth And One Day
No sooner come, but gone, and fal'n asleep,
Acquaintance short, yet parting caus'd us weep,
Three flours, two searcely blown, the last i'th' bud,
Cropt by th'Almighties hand; yet is he good,
With dreadful awe before him let's be mute,
Such was his will, but why, let's not dispute,
With humble hearts and mouths put in the dust,
Let's say he's merciful as well as just.
He will return, and make up all our losses,
And smile again, after our bitter crosses.
Go pretty babe, go rest with Sisters twain
Among the blest in endless joyes remain.

Spirit
Be still, thou unregenerate part,
Disturb no more my settled heart,
For I have vow'd (and so will do)
Thee as a foe still to pursue,
And combat with thee will and must
Until I see thee laid in th' dust.

Sister we are, yea twins we be,
Yet deadly feud 'twixt thee and me,
For from one father are we not.
Thou by old Adam wast begot,
But my arise is from above,
Whence my dear father I do love.
Thou speak'st me fair but hat'st me sore.
Thy flatt'ring shews I'll trust no more.
How oft thy slave hast thou me made
When I believ'd what thou hast said
And never had more cause of woe
Than when I did what thou bad'st do.
I'll stop mine ears at these thy charms
And count them for my deadly harms.
Thy sinful pleasures I do hate,
Thy riches are to me no bait.
Thine honours do, nor will I love,
For my ambition lies above.
My greatest honour it shall be
When I am victor over thee,
And Triumph shall, with laurel head,
When thou my Captive shalt be led.
How I do live, thou need'st not scoff,
For I have meat thou know'st not of.
The hidden Manna I do eat;
The word of life, it is my meat.
My thoughts do yield me more content
Than can thy hours in pleasure spent.
Nor are they shadows which I catch,
Nor fancies vain at which I snatch
But reach at things that are so high,
Beyond thy dull Capacity.
Eternal substance I do see
With which inriched I would be.
Mine eye doth pierce the heav'ns and see
What is Invisible to thee.
My garments are not silk nor gold,
Nor such like trash which Earth doth hold,
But Royal Robes I shall have on,
More glorious than the glist'ring Sun.
My Crown not Diamonds, Pearls, and gold,
But such as Angels' heads infold.
The City where I hope to dwell,
There's none on Earth can parallel.
The stately Walls both high and trong
Are made of precious Jasper stone,
The Gates of Pearl, both rich and clear,

And Angels are for Porters there.
The Streets thereof transparent gold
Such as no Eye did e're behold.
A Crystal River there doth run
Which doth proceed from the Lamb's Throne.
Of Life, there are the waters sure
Which shall remain forever pure.
Nor Sun nor Moon they have no need
For glory doth from God proceed.
No Candle there, nor yet Torch light,
For there shall be no darksome night.
From sickness and infirmity
Forevermore they shall be free.
Nor withering age shall e're come there,
But beauty shall be bright and clear.
This City pure is not for thee,
For things unclean there shall not be.
If I of Heav'n may have my fill,
Take thou the world, and all that will."

To Her Father With Some Verses
Most truly honoured, and as truly dear,
If worth in me or ought I do appear,
Who can of right better demand the same
Than may your worthy self from whom it came?
The principal might yield a greater sum,
Yet handled ill, amounts but to this crumb;
My stock's so small I know not how to pay,
My bond remains in force unto this day;
Yet for part payment take this simple mite,
Where nothing's to be had, kings loose their right.
Such is my debt I may not say forgive,
But as I can, I'll pay it while I live;
Such is my bond, none can discharge but I,
Yet paying is not paid until I die.

To Her Most Honoured Father Thomas Dudley Esq;
These Humbly Presented
Dear Sir of late delighted with the sight
Of your four Sisters cloth'd in black and white,
Of fairer Dames the Sun, ne'r saw the face;
Though made a pedestal for Adams Race;
Their worth so shines in these rich lines you show
Their paralels to finde I scarcely know
To climbe their Climes, I have nor strength nor skill

To mount so high requires an Eagles quill;
Yet view thereof did cause my thoughts to soar;
My lowly pen might wait upon these four
I bring my four times four, now meanly clad
To do their homage, unto yours, full glad:
Who for their Age, their worth and quality
Might seem of yours to claim precedency:
But by my humble hand, thus rudely pen'd
They are, your bounden handmaids to attend
These same are they, from whom we being have
These are of all, the Life, the Nurse, the Grave,
These are the hot, the cold, the moist, the dry,
That sink, that swim, that fill, that upwards fly,
Of these consists our bodies, Cloathes and Food,
The World, the useful, hurtful, and the good,
Sweet harmony they keep, yet jar oft times
Their discord doth appear, by these harsh rimes
Yours did contest for wealth, for Arts, for Age,
My first do shew their good, and then their rage.
My other foures do intermixed tell
Each others faults, and where themselves excell;
How hot and dry contend with moist and cold,
How Air and Earth no correspondence hold,
And yet in equal tempers, how they 'gree
How divers natures make one Unity
Something of all (though mean) I did intend
But fear'd you'ld judge Du Bartas was my friend
I honour him, but dare not wear his wealth
My goods are true (though poor) I love no stealth
But if I did I durst not send them you
Who must reward a Thief, but with his due.
I shall not need, mine innocence to clear
These ragged lines, will do't, when they appear:
On what they are, your mild aspect I crave
Accept my best, my worst vouchsafe a Grave.
From her that to your self, more duty owes
Then water in the boundess Ocean flows.

What God Is Like To Him I Serve
What God is like to him I serve,
What Saviour like to mine?
O, never let me from thee swerue,
For truly I am thine.
My thankfull mouth shall speak thy praise,
My Tongue shall talk of Thee:
On High my heart, O, doe thou raise,

For what thou'st done for me.
Goe, Worldlings, to your Vanities,
And heathen to your Gods;
Let them help in Adversities,
And sanctefye their rods.
My God he is not like to yours,
Your selves shall Judges bee;
I find his Love, I know his Pow'r,
A Succourer of mee.
He is not man that he should lye,
Nor son of man to vnsay;
His word he plighted hath on high,
And I shall liue for aye.
And for his sake that faithfull is,
That dy'd but now doth liue,
The first and last, that liues for aye,
Me lasting life shall giue.

www.ingramcontent.com/pod-product-compliance
Lightning Source LLC
Chambersburg PA
CBHW070112070426
42448CB00038B/2521